PARTICIPANT'S GUIDE

STEVEN FURTICK

with Eric Stanford

PARTICIPANT'S GUIDE

HEARING GOD'S VOICE
ABOVE ALL OTHERS

MULTNOMAH

CONTENTS

Calling All Chatterboxers

We demolish arguments and every pretension that
sets itself up against the knowledge of God, and
we take captive every thought to make it obedient
to Christ.

—2 Corinthians 10:5

The term *chatterbox* is my way of representing the lies we believe—lies of condemnation, fear, insecurity, and discouragement. This chatterbox is a voice that drones on and on inside
our heads, always intimidating, always insinuating. It wants to
wear us out until we have no idea what to do or how to answer
our growing list of doubts and deficiencies.

And it's not just what this chatter says that makes it danger-
ous. It's also what it keeps us from hearing.

See, most people go through life thinking God never speaks
to them when in fact He's always speaking. To everyone. Always directing. Sometimes warning. Sometimes affirming. But
we hear so little of what He says because our consciousness of
His voice is obscured by our mental static.

The Enemy's goal is to lure us into accepting his lies and limitations at face value. When we do, our faith only works in fits and starts. The lion's share of the good things that God has planned for us will remain out of reach. And the fruit we bear for God's glory will be minimal.

This means that when we learn how to crash the chatterbox—to overpower the Enemy's lies with God's truths—we're not simply learning to think more cheerful thoughts or adopt a more pleasant disposition or improve our lot in life. There's much more at stake than that. We're learning how to live in the spiritual power and effectiveness that God is holding out as a potential for each one of us.

And that's why I'm so glad you're using this *Crash the Chatterbox Participant's Guide*. It goes along with the *Crash the Chatterbox* DVD and makes it easy for you and a group of your friends to dive into the message that originated in my book of the same name. This participant's guide offers group discussion questions combined with a personal devotional guide and suggested action steps. It takes you from understanding to application so that you will begin to tune out the noisy lies in your head and tune in to the loving whispers of God.

It's time for you to become a chatterboxer. Fight back against the lies!

How to Use This Guide

This participant's guide is ideal for use...
- in adult or youth small groups, Bible studies, Sunday school classes, group counseling sessions, or ministry team meetings;
- on a church-wide basis along with a six-week series of sermons;
- for leadership training and personal development in business and community settings;
- as an individual or a couple.

However you choose to use this participant's guide, I hope you will maximize your experience by using it in conjunction with the book *Crash the Chatterbox* and the related DVD. There's also a challenge kit your church may find helpful. Check out crashthechatterbox.com for more information and updates.

If you're studying *Crash the Chatterbox* in an established group, you probably already have a clear sense of how your meetings should be organized and conducted to fit your context. But if you want a little more direction, here are some suggestions to get you started.

Group Use

If you're using this participant's guide in a small group, try to keep the size to no more than a dozen people so that everyone can share easily. You'll need to meet in a place where you can watch a DVD on a large screen and then sit comfortably to discuss the questions. There's enough material for about an hour of meeting time, though you can shrink or stretch it, depending on how your group manages the discussion time.

The Sessions

The sessions are designed to follow a simple format. You'll find an introduction you can read and an opening question that will help establish how the session topic applies to your life. Then you'll watch the video for that session, taking notes on your own as you watch. After that, you'll have an extended time of group discussion that breaks down the key idea for the session and starts to apply it to the participants' lives. Finally, you'll conclude your time with prayer.

Group Leader

One person should serve as the facilitator of the group sessions. This isn't a formal class, and there's no need for anyone to lecture or dominate the group, but someone should take responsibility for keeping the discussion rolling. See the Leader's Helps section at the back of this book for more information.

Community

Make these sessions opportunities for building relationships. Spend time getting to know other group members, encouraging and praying for one another. You may want to serve snacks. Consider sharing contact information and keeping in touch with one another between sessions.

After the Session

Each chapter ends with a section called After the Session, which includes a devotional guide and a suggested action step you can do at home in your free time. These are optional, of course, but they're also recommended. If you will give them a try, they will help you to further personalize the message of the *Crash the Chatterbox* DVD.

 This icon identifies a quote from the *Crash the Chatterbox* DVD.

 This icon identifies a quote from the book *Crash the Chatterbox*.

Recommended Reading Schedule for
Crash the Chatterbox

If you haven't already read the book *Crash the Chatterbox*, you may want to do so as you work your way through these sessions.

- Introduction and Chapter 1: read *before* Session 1.
- Chapters 2–4: read *before* Session 2.
- Chapters 5–7: read *before* Session 3.
- Chapters 8–10: read *before* Session 4.
- Chapters 11–13: read *before* Session 5.
- Conclusion: read *before* Session 6.

Introduction

The Chatterbox

This session's key idea: We can never tune out all the chatter—the lies in our minds—but we can learn to tune in to God's voice.

####

I read online that the average person has more than sixty thousand thoughts per day and over 80 percent of these thoughts are negative. Is that accurate? I don't know. But let's think together about the possibility that 80 percent of our thoughts are not only devoid of any power to help us but are also actively working against us. When we allow our thoughts to go unchecked, a steady drip of lies cements the wrong patterns within our minds, building a Berlin Wall of bad beliefs.

I wonder how much of its forty-eight-thousand-word quota your chatterbox has already filled today.

Did you hear it in the closet while you were getting dressed, telling you that it doesn't matter what you put on, that nothing will look good on you because you're too flabby, too bony, too pale, too old, or, in a single word, defective?

Did you hear it in the office where you work or in the home where you raise your children, telling you there's no point in trying so hard because no one notices anyway?

Do you hear it loudest at the end of the day, when mistakes and regrets and missteps can bounce around the room unobstructed by progress or perspective?

You sounded really stupid when…

How will you ever recover from…

Why would anybody want to be around a person like you, who…

God must be awfully disappointed in the way you…

We all have a chatterbox. How we respond to it will make the difference between a life spent floundering around in lies and regrets or a life that's making steady progress toward fulfilling God's desires for us.

Opening Question

Identify at least one of the lies you have been hearing in your mind lately. How has it affected your life?

I struggle with motherhood. When Paityn always wants to stay the night at my parents makes me feel like I'm failing. Which then puts the loud voices in my head.

Video Viewing

On the *Crash the Chatterbox* DVD, watch Video 1, titled "Introduction." While watching the video, use the spaces below to record the key points you hear or thoughts you want to remember.

Your Response to the Video

How we constantly have chatter in our heads, but God is speaking there too *2nd Corinthians 10:5 Take Captive of every thought to make it obedient to Christ.*

Once we expose our lies we introduce God's truth.

A plastic factory as an analogy for our minds putting out thoughts *Incredible analogy our mind is running full speed producing out thoughts, molding us. The more we think Christ-like the more we act like Christ. The more we think of the world the more we act like the world.*

If God is always speaking, it's not a matter of me getting Him to speak into my life. It's attuning my heart to His frequency so I can hear what He's been saying all along.

Being terrorized by thoughts

Being a good manager + making the right decisions. I'm always thinking. "What are the girls saying or thinking about me".

The four *Crash the Chatterbox* confessions

God says I am.
God says He will.
God says He has.
God says I can.

Group Discussion

1. *What challenged you most in Video 1, and why?*

Take captive of every thought + make it obedient

Taking a thought captive + detaining it. Every time a thought comes into the mind, I don't let it do whatever it wants to. Where did this thought come from? Interigate it!

2. Pastor Furtick compares our minds to a plastic factory because our minds are always producing thoughts either molded by the world or molded by God.

Describe what it's like for you to have a mental factory churning out good thoughts and bad thoughts all the time.

It's awful. It can keep me up at night. Stressing me out.

3. Just as negative chatter is always occurring inside our heads, God is always speaking to us.

How do you know He's speaking and not some other voice?

We have to line it with scripture. If it's truth, it's God. God is not negative.

Let God's truth speak to you. Let His word supersede what others have said, what you've been telling yourself. You might just discover that there's so much more God is calling you to do than what you're currently experiencing.

4. Read 2 Corinthians 10:1–6, and notice how Paul talks about managing our thought lives as a part of our ongoing spiritual war.

By the humility and gentleness of Christ, I appeal to you—I, Paul, who am "timid" when face to face with you, but "bold" toward you when away! I beg you that when I come I may not have to be as bold as I expect to be toward some people who think that we live by the standards of this world. For though we live in the world, we do not wage war as the world does. The weapons we fight with are not the weapons of the world. On the contrary, they have divine power to demolish strongholds. We demolish arguments and every pretension that sets itself up against the knowledge of God, and we take captive every thought to make it obedient to Christ. And we will be ready to punish every act of disobedience, once your obedience is complete.

What guidance was God trying to give you today that you didn't hear because it was buried by negative noise?

We don't have to let a thought into our minds. We can detain it and interrogate it. If it's from God, we can follow it. If it's not, we don't have to let it terrorize us.

How have thoughts terrorized you? How have your thoughts indirectly terrorized those closest to you?

I'm so obsessed with how I look + how I feel (healthy lfestyle) that I think sometimes I think it impacts Paityn's life in ways I'm blind to.

What do you think it means to take a thought captive? What do you think it means to make a thought obedient to Christ?

When I think "wow, I'm so fat, I wish I could lose 10 lbs." Instead, stop it before it continues + say I'm created in Gods image. I am fearfully + wonderfully made

5. Listening to the lies of the chatterbox hinders us from fulfilling God's calling on our lives.

What great things has God intended to do in your life that, until now, you've been unwilling or unable to press forward in because of the lies you've believed?

I find myself getting caught up in the worldly talk with the girls at work yet some days I try to witness. Not a good witness. I need to be consistent.

What is this costing you in terms of your joy?

By choosing to partake in their worldy
"talk" at work I'm feeling guilty
+ being a hypocrite.

What is it costing you in terms of your initiative?

I feel ashamed that I one day
talk the christian talk + the
next day I'm talking about banging
a guy.

*What is it costing those around you—people whom
God has been calling you to influence?*

Nan for instance may be
confused as to living the christian
lifestyle.

6. In the rest of this group study, we'll be looking at the
   four areas of lies: condemnation (*you are worthless and
   rejected*), fear (*the future is full of danger*), insecurity
   (*your mistakes disqualify you from God's love*), and
   discouragement (*you can't be the person you want to be
   or accomplish the things you want to accomplish*).

In which area would you say that you need the most help, and why?

fear + discouragement
fear - I'm always worrying about Paityn + the future.
discouragment - I feel I can't accomplish things because of the choices I've made in life

7. Our mental factory will never shut down, but we have more control over what the factory sends out than we may think.

What benefits are you looking forward to as you learn to subdue the lies in your mind and get better control over your thought life?

positivity state of mind.

Closing Prayer

Spend some time listening to prayer requests from the group. Pray for each other's needs and for progress in tuning out lies and tuning in to God's truth.

Doug doesn't let things at work bother him. Strenous work
Quiet time w/ Jesus

The *Crash the Chatterbox* Confessions

Confession 1: *God says I am.*

Overpowering the lies of the Enemy in your insecurities

Confession 2: *God says He will.*

Overpowering the lies of the Enemy in your fears

Confession 3: *God says He has.*

Overpowering the lies of the Enemy in your condemnation

Confession 4: *God says I can.*

Overpowering the lies of the Enemy in your discouragement

AFTER THE SESSION

On your own, use the following devotional guide and suggested action step to help make the key idea of Session 1 more personal and productive in your life.

My Time with God

Set aside several minutes to be alone with Christ in a quiet place, reading, thinking, praying, and journaling. First, read John 8:31–47, where Jesus talks about His truth and the Enemy's lies.

> To the Jews who had believed him, Jesus said, "If you hold to my teaching, you are really my disciples. Then you will know the truth, and the truth will set you free."
>
> They answered him, "We are Abraham's descendants and have never been slaves of anyone. How can you say that we shall be set free?"
>
> Jesus replied, "Very truly I tell you, everyone who sins is a slave to sin. Now a slave has no permanent place in the family, but a son belongs to it forever. So if the Son sets you free, you will be free indeed. I know that you are Abraham's descendants. Yet you are looking for a way to kill me, because you have no room for my word. I am telling you what I have seen in the Father's presence, and you are doing what you have heard from your father."

"Abraham is our father," they answered.

"If you were Abraham's children," said Jesus, "then you would do what Abraham did. As it is, you are looking for a way to kill me, a man who has told you the truth that I heard from God. Abraham did not do such things. You are doing the works of your own father."

"We are not illegitimate children," they protested. "The only Father we have is God himself."

Jesus said to them, "If God were your Father, you would love me, for I have come here from God. I have not come on my own; God sent me. Why is my language not clear to you? Because you are unable to hear what I say. You belong to your father, the devil, and you want to carry out your father's desires. He was a murderer from the beginning, not holding to the truth, for there is no truth in him. When he lies, he speaks his native language, for he is a liar and the father of lies. Yet because I tell the truth, you do not believe me! Can any of you prove me guilty of sin? If I am telling the truth, why don't you believe me? Whoever belongs to God hears what God says. The reason you do not hear is that you do not belong to God."

Did you note how seriously Jesus takes the issue of people making themselves friends of falsehood?

Consider these personal reflection questions:

- *How do I need Christ's truth to set me free?*
- *In what ways have I been complying with the devil by believing or repeating lies?*
- *What changes will I have to undergo if I want not just to believe but actually to live by the truthful affirmations of my heavenly Father?*

Spend time in prayer asking God to help you grow deaf to the devil's native language of lies and acquire fluency in the language of truth. If you feel you need to repent of anything, then repent. If you are moved to praise God, then praise Him.

Ask God what He wants to do in your life as you study *Crash the Chatterbox* and learn to hear His voice above all others. In the journaling space below, record any insights you feel you are receiving from Him:

My Action Step

Want to learn how to get better at crashing your chatterbox? Take the following survey. By phone, in person, or through e-mail, ask at least three mature Christians you know (not members of your study group) the following question:

How do you know when a thought in your head comes from God or when it's a lie that comes from some other source, such as the Enemy, your critics, your past, or your own faulty ideas?

List the names of the people you intend to survey:

1. _____

2. _____

3. _____

Identify tips, guidelines, or insights from their responses that can help you in your spiritual battles on the side of truth versus lies.

What I have learned about distinguishing lies from the truth:

Using your newfound knowledge, identify some of the most prevalent lies you believe the chatterbox has been telling you, along with truths God wants you to pay attention to. These are some of the issues you'll be dealing with in the rest of the *Crash the Chatterbox* experience.

Lies from the chatterbox I've been hearing in my mind:

Truths from God I've been hearing in my mind:

Insecurity
God Says I Am

*T*his session's key idea: The chatterbox says we are worthless and rejected, but God says we are His beloved children through Christ.

####

One of the most common ways the chatterbox tries to tear us down is by going straight to our identity, whispering things that make us insecure about who we are.

- *You're not good-looking or smart enough or talented enough to make it in this world.*
- *You'll never get victory over that sin.*
- *You're stuck and going nowhere in life.*
- *People don't like you.*
- *God doesn't like you much either.*

Any of that sound familiar?

That's why one of the most powerful confessions you can ever make starts like this: "God says I am _____." Then get busy learning how to fill in the blank. The Bible is full of vivid descriptions of the kinds of labels you should wear as God's child.

Once you've made the decision to build your self-assessment exclusively on God's Word, the chatterbox loses its ability to trash-talk you into submission. And the more adept you become at talking smack back to the chatterbox, the more ingrained the reality of who you are will become.

Crashing the chatterbox is about learning to say things like this—out loud—daily.

God says...

...I am His masterpiece.

...I am His workmanship.

...I am established.

...I am sealed with His promise.

...I am redeemed.

You confirm God's calling on your life when you learn to affirm your identity in Him. You activate your identity when you reject the lies of the chatterbox and instead walk according to specific redemptive truth.

- I don't like myself very much in this moment, but I am loved.
- I don't seem to be gaining much ground in this battle, but I am more than a conqueror.
- I don't have a lot of confidence in myself right now, but I am strong and courageous.

- I don't know how to fix this part of my life, but I am healed and whole.
- I don't know how long I'll continue to struggle with this sin, but I am forgiven and free.

You have every reason to feel secure. Because God says you are.

Opening Question

In what ways have you been feeling insecure lately?

I feel alone

Video Viewing

Watch Video 2, "Insecurity." While watching the video, use the spaces below to record the key points you hear or thoughts you want to remember.

Your Response to the Video

Interview with the chatterbox

Having security in God, not yourself

Sometimes we find our security in other people. Getting other peoples approval

The connection between circumstance and confidence

Instead of blaming my "tough season" on my failures (ie, divorce), I need to just be confident that God loves me & forgives me even with divorce

Looking for approval from God, not other people

We don't need some one elses approval we already have Gods. We just have to accept it.

Group Discussion

1. *What challenged you most in Video 2, and why?*

blaming my divorce on myself + how I'm alone because of the circumstances I've mad

2. Video 2 begins with Pastor Furtick interviewing the chatterbox, a character we'll meet in other videos on the DVD.

What messages of insecurity did you recognize in the chatterbox's examples—things you've heard in your own head?

No one will ever love you, you're too hard to love.

3. Pastor Furtick says arrogance and insecurity are two heads of the same self-centered monster. Just like pride, insecurity makes our thoughts about ourselves all the time.

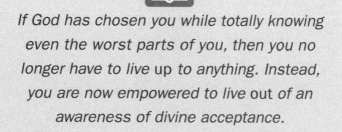

If God has chosen you while totally knowing even the worst parts of you, then you no longer have to live up to anything. Instead, you are now empowered to live out of an awareness of divine acceptance.

How has your insecurity led you to focus on yourself?
What things would be better for you to focus on
instead?

I'm alway feeling "poor me"!

4. When we are insecure, feeling like we're just not good
   enough, it is an insult to God because it implies
   criticism of the Creator who made us.

How do you think God feels about your feelings of
insecurity?

He feels sad. God doesn't create junk

5. Our worth is like a computer file stored in the cloud
   instead of on a personal computer. In other words, our
   worth is not in us; it's in Christ.

How would you describe your value in Christ?

He died for my sins. He paid the ultimate price for me.

6. Most of us feel confident if our circumstances are good but insecure if our circumstances are bad.

   Describe a way that your circumstances have dictated your confidence (or lack thereof). When work is rough, come home + Paityn doesn't want to stay the night with me, I instantly think of course because I'm a failure.

7. Read Romans 8:31–39.

   > *If God is for us, who can be against us? He who did not spare his own Son, but gave him up for us all— how will he not also, along with him, graciously give us all things? Who will bring any charge against those whom God has chosen? It is God who justifies. Who then is the one who condemns? No one. Christ Jesus who died—more than that, who was raised to life—is*

What's required for me to access what I have in God, and who I really am in Him, is a connection through the Holy Spirit.

---

at the right hand of God and is also interceding for us.
Who shall separate us from the love of Christ? Shall
trouble or hardship or persecution or famine or
nakedness or danger or sword? As it is written:

> *"For your sake we face death all day long;*
> *we are considered as sheep to be slaughtered."*

No, in all these things we are more than conquerors
through him who loved us. For I am convinced that
neither death nor life, neither angels nor demons,
neither the present nor the future, nor any powers,
neither height nor depth, nor anything else in all
creation, will be able to separate us from the love of
God that is in Christ Jesus our Lord.

Nothing can separate us from the love of God. If we are
in Christ, we are accepted and loved—permanently.

What would it take for you to move from having your
confidence depend on your circumstances to having
your confidence rest on your secure relationship with
God?

Be in the word every. single. day

*What dangers would you face if you were to forget
who you are in Christ?* I was running towards
men, I was running towards compliments,
from men, anything that made me
feel good other than Christ.

8. Read Matthew 3:13–4:11, which describes both the
   baptism of Jesus and the temptation that immediately
   followed.

*Jesus came from Galilee to the Jordan to be baptized
by John. But John tried to deter him, saying, "I need
to be baptized by you, and do you come to me?"*

*Jesus replied, "Let it be so now; it is proper for us
to do this to fulfill all righteousness." Then John
consented.*

*As soon as Jesus was baptized, he went up out of
the water. At that moment heaven was opened, and
he saw the Spirit of God descending like a dove and
alighting on him. And a voice from heaven said,
"This is my Son, whom I love; with him I am well
pleased."*

*Then Jesus was led by the Spirit into the wilder-
ness to be tempted by the devil. After fasting forty days
and forty nights, he was hungry. The tempter came to*

him and said, "If you are the Son of God, tell these stones to become bread."

Jesus answered, "It is written: 'Man shall not live on bread alone, but on every word that comes from the mouth of God.'"

Then the devil took him to the holy city and had him stand on the highest point of the temple. "If you are the Son of God," he said, "throw yourself down. For it is written:

> *"'He will command his angels concerning you,*
>> *and they will lift you up in their hands,*
>>> *so that you will not strike your foot against a*
>>>> *stone.'"*

Jesus answered him, "It is also written: 'Do not put the Lord your God to the test.'"

Again, the devil took him to a very high mountain and showed him all the kingdoms of the world and their splendor. "All this I will give you," he said, "if you will bow down and worship me."

Jesus said to him, "Away from me, Satan! For it is written: 'Worship the Lord your God, and serve him only.'"

Then the devil left him, and angels came and attended him.

Jesus faced the chatter of temptation in the wilderness. But He could resist it because He already had a foundation of affirmation when the Father spoke His approval of Jesus at the baptism.

How has the Father given you His affirmation through your faith in Christ? How can this affirmation help you turn down the volume on the chatterbox? On good days, I'm thankful for my divorce + parenting because I feel like I was created to help others through these times + have hope. I was created for so much more in Him.

9. We have to find ways daily to be baptized in God's affirmation. Rebuke Satan before even Stepping out of bed. Thank God for preparing and attacking my battles. Memorize verses.

> What God is interested in is a confidence that rests in something different than circumstance.

What are some ways that help you remember God's approval? Scripture

Remembering He died for me.

How can His approval help you in your battles with insecurity right now?

Memorizing scripture,
remembering HIS promises,
rebuking Satan,
Staying in his word

Closing Prayer

As a group, pray for God to *reveal* His love and acceptance for all of you in Christ and enable you to better *receive* this love.

AFTER THE SESSION

Use the following devotional guide and suggested action step to help make the key idea of Session 2 more personal and productive in your life.

My Time with God

Read Luke 1:26–56, the story of Mary's humble security in God when told of the amazing way God was going to work through her life.

> *In the sixth month of Elizabeth's pregnancy, God sent the angel Gabriel to Nazareth, a town in Galilee, to a virgin pledged to be married to a man named Joseph, a descendant of David. The virgin's name was Mary. The angel went to her and said, "Greetings, you who are highly favored! The Lord is with you."*
>
> *Mary was greatly troubled at his words and wondered what kind of greeting this might be. But the angel said to her, "Do not be afraid, Mary; you have found favor with God. You will conceive and give birth to a son, and you are to call him Jesus. He will be great and will be called the Son of the Most High. The Lord God will give him the throne of his father David, and he will reign over Jacob's descendants forever; his kingdom will never end."*
>
> *"How will this be," Mary asked the angel, "since I am a virgin?"*

The angel answered, "The Holy Spirit will come on you, and the power of the Most High will overshadow you. So the holy one to be born will be called the Son of God. Even Elizabeth your relative is going to have a child in her old age, and she who was said to be unable to conceive is in her sixth month. For no word from God will ever fail."

"I am the Lord's servant," Mary answered. "May your word to me be fulfilled." Then the angel left her.

At that time Mary got ready and hurried to a town in the hill country of Judea, where she entered Zechariah's home and greeted Elizabeth. When Elizabeth heard Mary's greeting, the baby leaped in her womb, and Elizabeth was filled with the Holy Spirit. In a loud voice she exclaimed: "Blessed are you among women, and blessed is the child you will bear! But why am I so favored, that the mother of my Lord should come to me? As soon as the sound of your greeting reached my ears, the baby in my womb leaped for joy. Blessed is she who has believed that the Lord would fulfill his promises to her!"

And Mary said:

"My soul glorifies the Lord
    and my spirit rejoices in God my Savior,
for he has been mindful
    of the humble state of his servant.
From now on all generations will call me blessed,

for the Mighty One has done great things for me—
　　holy is his name.
His mercy extends to those who fear him,
　　from generation to generation.
He has performed mighty deeds with his arm;
　　he has scattered those who are proud in their inmost
　　　　thoughts.
He has brought down rulers from their thrones
　　but has lifted up the humble.
He has filled the hungry with good things
　　but has sent the rich away empty.
He has helped his servant Israel,
　　remembering to be merciful
to Abraham and his descendants forever,
　　just as he promised our ancestors."

　　Mary stayed with Elizabeth for about three months and
then returned home.

This young woman made the transition from stunned to submissive to thankful with extraordinary grace.

Consider these personal reflection questions:

- *How might the Enemy have attacked Mary's sense of security when she found out that she would bear the Son of God?*

- *Judging by what she said to Elizabeth, what identity did Mary embrace?*
- *What is there in her response to her calling that I would like to copy?*

Think about God's calling (or callings) on your life as you understand them at this point. What reasons do you have to believe that you can be faithful in these callings, not because of who you are, but because of who God is? Pray and ask Him to help you live out your confidence in Him.

In the journaling space below, record your thoughts and insights:

My Action Step

Read each of the following Bible passages. Then use them to complete a "God says I am…" sentence that helps define your identity in Christ. The first one is done for you as an example.

Be strong and courageous. Do not be afraid or terrified because of them, for the LORD your God goes with you; he will never leave you nor forsake you. (Deuteronomy 31:6)

• God says I am <u>strong and courageous because He is with me</u>.

I praise you because I am fearfully and wonderfully made. (Psalm 139:14)

• God says I am _____.

You are the salt of the earth…. You are the light of the world. (Matthew 5:13–14)

• God says I am _____.

As the Father has loved me, so have I loved you. Now remain in my love. (John 15:9)

• God says I am _____.

I no longer call you servants, because a servant does not know his master's business. Instead, I have called you friends. (John 15:15)

• God says I am _____.

You have been set free from sin and have become slaves to righteousness. (Romans 6:18)

• God says I am _____.

If we are children, then we are heirs—heirs of God and coheirs with Christ. (Romans 8:17)

• God says I am _____.

We are more than conquerors through him who loved us. (Romans 8:37)

• God says I am _____.

It is God who makes both us and you stand firm in Christ. (2 Corinthians 1:21)

• God says I am _____.

If anyone is in Christ, the new creation has come: The old has gone, the new is here! (2 Corinthians 5:17)

• God says I am _____.

In Christ Jesus you are all children of God through faith, for all of you who were baptized into Christ have clothed yourselves with Christ. (Galatians 3:26–27)

• God says I am _____.

He chose us in him before the creation of the world to be holy and blameless in his sight. (Ephesians 1:4)

• God says I am _____.

God raised us up with Christ and seated us with him in the heavenly realms in Christ Jesus. (Ephesians 2:6)

• God says I am _____.

We are God's handiwork, created in Christ Jesus to do good works, which God prepared in advance for us to do. (Ephesians 2:10)

• God says I am _____.

You are no longer foreigners and strangers, but fellow citizens with God's people and also members of his household. (Ephesians 2:19)

• God says I am _____.

He has rescued us from the dominion of darkness and brought us into the kingdom of the Son he loves, in whom we have redemption, the forgiveness of sins. (Colossians 1:13–14)

• God says I am _____.

When you were dead in your sins and in the uncircumcision of your flesh, God made you alive with Christ. (Colossians 2:13)

• God says I am _____.

You died, and your life is now hidden with Christ in God. (Colossians 3:3)

• God says I am _____.

You are a chosen people, a royal priesthood, a holy nation, God's special possession, that you may declare the praises of him who called you out of darkness into his wonderful light. (1 Peter 2:9)

• God says I am _____.

We know that anyone born of God does not continue to sin; the One who was born of God keeps them safe, and the evil one cannot harm them. (1 John 5:18)

• God says I am _____.

If you want more Bible passages that affirm how God sees you, go online and use the search phrase "identity in Christ." See what Bible verses this search leads you to, and add them to the list.

Circle one or more verses that best minister the affirmation of the Father to you. Commit them to memory so you can draw them out when needed to resist the Enemy, just as Jesus did during His temptation.

Fear

God Says He Will

his session's key idea: The chatterbox says the future is full of danger, but God says He will preserve and protect us.

Fear is both a global and a personal experience for all of us. We fear stuff we can't control, and at the same time we tremble at the things we can control. We fear terrorist attacks and breast cancer. We fear opening e-mails that might contain extra work from our boss or a hurtful remark from our sister.

This kind of fear doesn't just go away. In fact, if left alone, it tends to compound, spread, and destroy. Little fears can combine to form levels of anxiety and terror that will annihilate our awareness of the presence of God. Fear pushes us around like Nelson bullies Bart Simpson and Milhouse, and it holds a Keep Out sign over the adventure, wonder, and even simple confidence God has called us to experience.

I love the way the Amplified Bible translates 1 John 4:18: "There is no fear in love, but full-grown love turns fear out of doors and expels every trace of terror!" When I read that, I picture fear standing at the doorway of our destinies, daring us to step inside. I can hear all the different lines the chatterbox uses to intimidate us when we're on the verge of doing something God has told us to do.

The fact is, we'll never hear God's voice above all the others if we're tuned in to the frequencies of fear. If we're going to put our roots down deeper and deeper into the soil of who God says we are, we'll have to learn to push past all the varieties of heart-hardening fears.

As I'm sure you already know, fear is an insidious force that has silenced the dreams and sabotaged the development of so many of God's children. But there is a confession that gives us access to a much greater force—the counteractive force of faith.

No matter what happens to us, *God says He will...*

...still be the cornerstone of our lives.

...protect us.

One great thing about experiencing your greatest fear is you see that, even after the devil has done his worst to you, you still have a faithful God who will uphold you in ways you didn't know.

...restore our joy.

...give us peace that passes understanding.

...put us back together.

...open our eyes to new opportunities.

...lead us to triumph.

Opening Question

What fears haunt you?

Video Viewing

Watch Video 3, "Fear." While watching the video, use the spaces below to record the key points you hear or thoughts you want to remember.

Your Response to the Video

Monologue by the chatterbox

Wading into the deep waters of our fears

God opening the eyes of Elisha's servant

Drawing a second circle

Trying to live mistake-free lives

Getting outside our comfort zones and being vulnerable

Group Discussion

1. *What challenged you most in Video 3, and why?*

2. *In the chatterbox's monologue about inspiring regrets, what sounded familiar to you?*

Some people say that we should never experience fear or accept fear. The problem a lot of times is that we don't go deep enough into our fear.

3. Pastor Furtick says that, instead of ignoring our fears, we should go deeper into them. Pick one of your fears and then answer...

What is the worst that could happen if that fear is realized? What could God do for you even in that situation?

4. Read 2 Kings 6:8–23, the story of a battle in which seeing and not seeing play surprising roles.

Now the king of Aram was at war with Israel. After conferring with his officers, he said, "I will set up my camp in such and such a place."

The man of God sent word to the king of Israel: "Beware of passing that place, because the Arameans are going down there." So the king of Israel checked on the place indicated by the man of God. Time and again Elisha warned the king, so that he was on his guard in such places.

This enraged the king of Aram. He summoned his

officers and demanded of them, "Tell me! Which of us is on the side of the king of Israel?"

"None of us, my lord the king," said one of his officers, "but Elisha, the prophet who is in Israel, tells the king of Israel the very words you speak in your bedroom."

"Go, find out where he is," the king ordered, "so I can send men and capture him." The report came back: "He is in Dothan." Then he sent horses and chariots and a strong force there. They went by night and surrounded the city.

When the servant of the man of God got up and went out early the next morning, an army with horses and chariots had surrounded the city. "Oh no, my lord! What shall we do?" the servant asked.

"Don't be afraid," the prophet answered. "Those who are with us are more than those who are with them."

And Elisha prayed, "Open his eyes, LORD, so that he may see." Then the LORD opened the servant's eyes, and he looked and saw the hills full of horses and chariots of fire all around Elisha.

As the enemy came down toward him, Elisha prayed to the LORD, "Strike this army with blindness." So he struck them with blindness, as Elisha had asked.

Elisha told them, "This is not the road and this is

not the city. Follow me, and I will lead you to the man you are looking for." And he led them to Samaria.

After they entered the city, Elisha said, "LORD, open the eyes of these men so they can see." Then the LORD opened their eyes and they looked, and there they were, inside Samaria.

When the king of Israel saw them, he asked Elisha, "Shall I kill them, my father? Shall I kill them?"

"Do not kill them," he answered. "Would you kill those you have captured with your own sword or bow? Set food and water before them so that they may eat and drink and then go back to their master." So he prepared a great feast for them, and after they had finished eating and drinking, he sent them away, and they returned to their master. So the bands from Aram stopped raiding Israel's territory.

You either kick fear out *of your heart or it will* keep you out *of the places God has prepared for you.*

The incident of Elisha's servant seeing the angelic armies shows us that God's protection is always there. We just need to have a new perspective in order to see it.

How are you beginning to see the presence and might of God in the problem areas of your life?

5. On a piece of paper, draw a circle and label it with a *C*, representing the things you can control. Then draw a larger circle around it, representing the totality of your life under the control of God. Inside that larger circle write some of your biggest current fears. Show the paper to the group and explain what you've written.

Are you able to trust that God can handle all the potential dangers that are outside your control? Explain.

6. Read the parable of the bags of gold in Matthew
   25:14–30.

*[The kingdom of heaven] will be like a man going on
a journey, who called his servants and entrusted his
wealth to them. To one he gave five bags of gold, to
another two bags, and to another one bag, each
according to his ability. Then he went on his journey.
The man who had received five bags of gold went at
once and put his money to work and gained five bags
more. So also, the one with two bags of gold gained
two more. But the man who had received one bag
went off, dug a hole in the ground and hid his master's
money.*

*After a long time the master of those servants
returned and settled accounts with them. The man
who had received five bags of gold brought the other
five. "Master," he said, "you entrusted me with five
bags of gold. See, I have gained five more."*

*His master replied, "Well done, good and faithful
servant! You have been faithful with a few things; I
will put you in charge of many things. Come and share
your master's happiness!"*

*The man with two bags of gold also came. "Mas-
ter," he said, "you entrusted me with two bags of gold;
see, I have gained two more."*

His master replied, *"Well done, good and faithful servant! You have been faithful with a few things; I will put you in charge of many things. Come and share your master's happiness!"*

Then the man who had received one bag of gold came. "Master," he said, "I knew that you are a hard man, harvesting where you have not sown and gathering where you have not scattered seed. So I was afraid and went out and hid your gold in the ground. See, here is what belongs to you."

His master replied, "You wicked, lazy servant! So you knew that I harvest where I have not sown and gather where I have not scattered seed? Well then, you should have put my money on deposit with the bankers, so that when I returned I would have received it back with interest.

"So take the bag of gold from him and give it to the one who has ten bags. For whoever has will be given more, and they will have an abundance. Whoever does

When the chatter starts, take it as an announcement that God is about to do something awesome in your life.

not have, even what they have will be taken from them. And throw that worthless servant outside, into the darkness, where there will be weeping and gnashing of teeth."

How does this story illustrate the truth that Jesus was more critical of lacking faith than of making a mistake?

Which servant are you more like, and why?

7. It's a mistake (not to mention futile) to try to lead a mistake-free life, because that is not where our focus is supposed to be.

   Have you been trying to live a mistake-free life? If so, how?

How do you tell the difference between faithful risk taking and foolish recklessness?

8. Mistakes are never good in themselves, yet God can use us despite, and often because of, our mistakes. Think about a mistake you're fearful of making. Then answer...

   If you were to make that kind of mistake but didn't give up on following God's call, how might He be able to use you anyway?

9. When we stay inside our comfort zones, we're never able to find out what God can do beyond us.

   What might you be missing out on by hiding in your comfort zone?

10. Pastor Furtick says we should look at fear as a sign not that we've gone too far but that we need to keep going further in response to God. Why? Because the very fact that the Enemy attacks us through our fears shows we are in a position to do something he doesn't want.

If you saw your fear as a sign not to put on the brakes but to go full speed ahead, how would that change your choices?

Closing Prayer

Get together in groups of two or three, share your fears, and pray for one another. Agree to keep on praying during the days ahead for God to strengthen each one's faith and give you a holy boldness.

Use the following devotional guide and suggested action step to help make the key idea of Session 3 more personal and productive in your life.

My Time with God

Read Mark 4:35–41, a story of Jesus on the Sea of Galilee.

> When evening came, [Jesus] said to his disciples, "Let us go over to the other side." Leaving the crowd behind, they took him along, just as he was, in the boat. There were also other boats with him. A furious squall came up, and the waves broke over the boat, so that it was nearly swamped. Jesus was in the stern, sleeping on a cushion. The disciples woke him and said to him, "Teacher, don't you care if we drown?"
>
> He got up, rebuked the wind and said to the waves, "Quiet! Be still!" Then the wind died down and it was completely calm.
>
> He said to his disciples, "Why are you so afraid? Do you still have no faith?"
>
> They were terrified and asked each other, "Who is this? Even the wind and the waves obey him!"

Here, fear and faith go up and down like waves, and a powerful storm meets its match in the Lord of creation.

Consider these personal reflection questions:

- *What is the storm in my life right now? What kind of fear is it inspiring in me?*
- *Am I being faithless, like the disciples? If so, how?*
- *What great and powerful things might Jesus want to do in response to my storm?*

Go ahead and wake up Jesus to ask Him to calm your storm. You've probably already done that more than once, but that's okay—the Bible encourages persistent prayer (see Luke 18:1–8). Just be sure you are praying with trust in your heart that God will do what is best from His eternal perspective. The waves may not subside instantly, and your boat may suffer loss, but in the end you will get safely to the other side, and God will complete His purpose for your life.

After your prayer time, in the journaling space below, record your thoughts and insights.

My Action Step

Identify a fear that is holding you back from being fully faithful to God. Then choose one positive step you can take in the direction of obedience to God despite your fear—and act on it. For example, if you feel God is calling you to teach a group of teens but you have a crippling shyness about being the center of attention, start small by initiating a discipling relationship with one or two students.

My fear:

My first step of obedience:

You may wish to ask someone to pray with you and give you support as you act in defiance of your fear. Be sure to share your victory with this person and give God the glory.

Remember, "there is no fear in love, but full-grown love turns fear out of doors and expels every trace of terror!" (1 John 4:18, AMP). Let the maturing love of Christ within you send fear racing to the exit doors of your heart.

Condemnation

God Says He Has

his session's key idea: The chatterbox says our wrongdoing disqualifies us from God's love, but God says He has forgiven and accepted us through Christ.

####

The chatterbox speaks lies of insecurity and fear, as we've already seen. He also speaks lies of condemnation, telling us how bad we are and how much God must hate us and how we ought to hate ourselves. These are incredibly destructive lies. Except, since we're sinners, they're really more like half truths.

Here's what the voice of condemnation sounds like: *This stuff you believe about how you're filled with the Spirit is a lot of hocus-pocus, isn't it? If not, why isn't it working for you? Even your good deeds aren't as good as you would have others believe. If you're filled with the Spirit, why would you* [insert recent act of selfishness]*? And if you're really a follower of Christ, then why wouldn't you* [insert recent missed opportunity to glorify God]*?*

The chatterbox accuses us of all kinds of shortcomings—all the ways our hearts are incongruent with God's Word, all the old habits that persist in our daily lives. And the worst part about this chatter is that so much of it is on target! We really have messed up.

We can't un-sin. We can only repent. And every time we do, we find that God doesn't leverage our sins against us like the chatterbox does. His kindness leads us to repentance. He leverages grace against our sin to bring us to deeper dependency upon Him.

So we need to flip the script on the chatterbox.

When the Enemy starts bombarding our minds with condemnations—about events that happened seconds ago or decades ago—we can remind him of what God did and what He has promised to do for us. The relevant confession here is "God says He has…"

God says He has forgiven us. And His grace is cleansing us.

God says He has called us. And His mercy is keeping us.

God says He has rescued our lives from the pit. And His kindness is crowning us with love and compassion.

Opening Question

What are some of the condemning messages you hear inside your head?

Video Viewing

Watch Video 4, "Condemnation." While watching the video, use the spaces below to record the key points you hear or thoughts you want to remember.

Your Response to the Video

The interview with the chatterbox

The Christmas apocalypse—condemning messages flying around like packing peanuts

---

The chatterbox takes what is glorious and ruins it. But God takes what is ruined and turns it into something glorious.

How the Enemy diminishes the seriousness of sin when he's tempting us and magnifies it after we've fallen

The three *p*'s of condemnation

How God uses someone who has sinned

How God shapes our scars to display His power

Group Discussion

1. *What challenged you most in Video 4, and why?*

2. Listening to the chatterbox insult Pastor Furtick on the video is painful because we've all allowed similar thoughts to enter our minds.

   What sounded familiar to you in the tone or content of the chatterbox's degrading mockery?

3. Many of us want to wait until we feel forgiven before we move on to what God has called us to. The problem with this approach is that while we're waiting to feel forgiven about one thing, we'll do something else that makes us feel guilty. And then we'll *never* get anywhere.

Is your sense of guilt paralyzing you? Explain.

4. The foundation for coming to God is never *how we feel about ourselves.* It's *what Christ has actually done for us* on the cross, making forgiveness a reality for us as we trust in Him.

   Tell about the time when you first put your faith in Christ for salvation. What assurance do you have that you are forgiven?

5. When he's tempting us, the Enemy plays down the seriousness of sin to try to get us to take the bait. Then after we've sinned, he turns around and plays up the awfulness of what we've done to try to put distance between God and us.

How could you beat the Enemy at his own game by using the voice of condemnation, not to spur you to run away from God, but to make you run faster to Him for forgiveness and reconciliation? Give an example of how that could work.

6. Pastor Furtick says that condemnation is a counterfeit of conviction. Condemnation makes us think our sin is permanent (eliminating any hope for change), personalized (tainting our very identity), and pervasive (extending to every part of our lives). Conviction, on the other hand, simply tells us that we've done wrong and then lovingly draws us to God for forgiveness.

> *The quickest way that you can disrupt God's perfect process in your life is to try to present to others an image of yourself that is perfect.*

How have you experienced the difference between the Enemy's condemnation of you and the Holy Spirit's conviction within your heart?

7. Of course God still uses someone who struggles with sin. He doesn't have anybody else to use.

   Do you ever worry that your struggles with sin disqualify you from God's service? Explain.

8. Read 2 Corinthians 11:16–12:10, where the apostle Paul employed a surprising tactic to defend himself against charges that he was inferior to some ironically named "super-apostles."

   Let no one take me for a fool. But if you do, then tolerate me just as you would a fool, so that I may do a little boasting. In this self-confident boasting I am not

talking as the Lord would, but as a fool. Since many
are boasting in the way the world does, I too will
boast. You gladly put up with fools since you are so
wise! In fact, you even put up with anyone who
enslaves you or exploits you or takes advantage of you
or puts on airs or slaps you in the face. To my shame I
admit that we were too weak for that!

Whatever anyone else dares to boast about—I am
speaking as a fool—I also dare to boast about. Are
they Hebrews? So am I. Are they Israelites? So am I.
Are they Abraham's descendants? So am I. Are they
servants of Christ? (I am out of my mind to talk like
this.) I am more. I have worked much harder, been in
prison more frequently, been flogged more severely,
and been exposed to death again and again. Five times
I received from the Jews the forty lashes minus one.
Three times I was beaten with rods, once I was pelted
with stones, three times I was shipwrecked, I spent a
night and a day in the open sea, I have been constantly
on the move. I have been in danger from rivers, in

*Everything changed for me when I realized that
you don't have to feel forgiven to be forgiven.*

danger from bandits, in danger from my fellow Jews, in danger from Gentiles; in danger in the city, in danger in the country, in danger at sea; and in danger from false believers. I have labored and toiled and have often gone without sleep; I have known hunger and thirst and have often gone without food; I have been cold and naked. Besides everything else, I face daily the pressure of my concern for all the churches. Who is weak, and I do not feel weak? Who is led into sin, and I do not inwardly burn?

If I must boast, I will boast of the things that show my weakness. The God and Father of the Lord Jesus, who is to be praised forever, knows that I am not lying. In Damascus the governor under King Aretas had the city of the Damascenes guarded in order to arrest me. But I was lowered in a basket from a window in the wall and slipped through his hands.

I must go on boasting. Although there is nothing to be gained, I will go on to visions and revelations from the Lord. I know a man in Christ who fourteen years ago was caught up to the third heaven. Whether it was in the body or out of the body I do not know—God knows. And I know that this man—whether in the body or apart from the body I do not know, but God knows—was caught up to paradise and heard inexpressible things, things that no one is permitted to tell.

I will boast about a man like that, but I will not boast about myself, except about my weaknesses. Even if I should choose to boast, I would not be a fool, because I would be speaking the truth. But I refrain, so no one will think more of me than is warranted by what I do or say, or because of these surpassingly great revelations. Therefore, in order to keep me from becoming conceited, I was given a thorn in my flesh, a messenger of Satan, to torment me. Three times I pleaded with the Lord to take it away from me. But he said to me, "My grace is sufficient for you, for my power is made perfect in weakness." Therefore I will boast all the more gladly about my weaknesses, so that Christ's power may rest on me. That is why, for Christ's sake, I delight in weaknesses, in insults, in hardships, in persecutions, in difficulties. For when I am weak, then I am strong.

Paul defended himself against the so-called super-apostles, not by boasting about his credentials, but by boasting about his outward hardships and inward struggles.

How has God proved Himself strong in your life even when you have been weak?

9. When we're real about our struggles with sin—not excusing them but not denying them either—it gives other people a pattern to follow in taking their sin to God for redemption. Therefore, we should not try to hide our struggles from ourselves or other people.

   How could being real about our sin actually improve our witness for Christ to nonbelievers? Give an example if you have one.

10. God has a way of shaping our spiritual scars to reveal His glory to the world.

While the chatterbox reminds us of our wrongs by showing us our shame over and over again, the Spirit convicts us of our sin by reminding us of our righteousness.

How do you think God wants to turn your past mistakes and sins into something glorious?

Closing Prayer

Intercede for one another about your struggles with sin. Ask God to forgive the sin, strengthen each one in holiness, and glorify Himself by using the group members even in their imperfections.

Use the following devotional guide and suggested action step to help make the key idea of Session 4 more personal and productive in your life.

My Time with God

Read Luke 22:54–62, which records what must have been the most cheek-reddening incident of Peter's life. This shameful event happened on the night that a squad of soldiers came to arrest Jesus.

> *Seizing [Jesus], they led him away and took him into the house of the high priest. Peter followed at a distance. And when some there had kindled a fire in the middle of the courtyard and had sat down together, Peter sat down with them. A servant girl saw him seated there in the firelight. She looked closely at him and said, "This man was with him."*
>
> *But he denied it. "Woman, I don't know him," he said.*
>
> *A little later someone else saw him and said, "You also are one of them."*
>
> *"Man, I am not!" Peter replied.*
>
> *About an hour later another asserted, "Certainly this fellow was with him, for he is a Galilean."*
>
> *Peter replied, "Man, I don't know what you're talking about!" Just as he was speaking, the rooster crowed. The Lord*

turned and looked straight at Peter. Then Peter remembered
the word the Lord had spoken to him: "Before the rooster
crows today, you will disown me three times." And he went
outside and wept bitterly.

Earlier that night Peter had sworn his allegiance to Jesus, and Jesus had kicked the legs out from under the disciple's smug self-confidence by foretelling that Peter would deny Him before the morning's first cock crow (see Luke 22:31–34). So, for Peter, the sound of *cock-a-doodle-doo* was a horrible message of condemnation: *You have denied Jesus at His moment of greatest peril, just as He said you would!* But in that moment Jesus gave him a look of love to begin drawing him toward a place of forgiveness and acceptance.

Consider these personal reflection questions:

- *How have I betrayed Jesus by my thoughts, words, or actions? How does the Enemy remind me over and over again of my shame?*
- *If I could see the expression in Jesus's eyes as he looks at me right now, what would it show me?*
- *What does God want me to do with the load of guilt I've been bearing?*

In a time of prayer, ask God to show you the realities of righteousness that He wants you to remember and the sins of the past He wants you to forget. Seek His help to put sin, guilt, shame, and condemnation behind you.

Journal your thoughts here:

My Action Step

On slips of paper, write out the condemning messages that the chatterbox has been filling your mind with most persistently. Or tear out this page and use it for the same purpose. For example, you might write (from the chatterbox's point of view) "You are a hypocrite" or "You are a failure as a parent."

Condemnation: "You _____."

Condemnation: "You _____."

Condemnation: "You _____."

Condemnation: "You _____."

Condemnation: "You _____."

Condemnation: "You _____."

After you've written these condemnations, put the paper in an envelope and write "Return to sender" on it. Then burn it. Or rip it into tiny pieces and drop them in the trash. Or run it through a shredder. Or tie it to a rock and throw it into a body of water. The point is to vividly symbolize your rejection of false condemnation.

Granted, this act won't prevent messages of condemnation from slipping into your mind again. But it *will* give you a reminder that these messages don't have to have any power over you.

"There is now no condemnation for those who are in Christ Jesus" (Romans 8:1).

Discouragement
God Says I Can

This session's key idea: The chatterbox says we can't accomplish the things we want to do, but God says we can do all things through Christ who strengthens us.

####

If you are a believer who hopes to accomplish the will of God for your life, you have to defy the inertia of internal discouragement.

Discouragement shows up in multiple ways. It can set in because of what others say or don't say, what they do or don't do. It can hit as hard when we're winning as when we're losing. Sometimes it comes like a flood; sometimes it drips incessantly.

Regardless of how or when it arrives, discouragement always displaces hope and leaves you feeling something like this: *It's not working, so what's the point?*

You don't have what it takes to ace this class, so why keep cracking the books?

The boss doesn't like you. Just punch the clock and forget trying to get ahead.

Those love handles will never melt away no matter how much time you spend on the elliptical.

Forget about resolving yet again to quit. You know you'll never beat it.

The relationship is ruined. What's the point of trying to make it work?

Disappointed expectations, when full grown, give birth to chronic discouragement. If you allow this discouragement to run rampant in your life, you'll lose all hope.

So when the internal dialogue of discouragement starts in your heart, remember: The Enemy's goal goes way beyond temporarily putting you in a bad mood. He's trying to talk you out of trusting God's plan for your life at a foundational level.

Rejecting the chatter of discouragement and persisting instead in the purposes of God require choosing to believe what He has said, whether you can hear it now or not. And what did He say? He said, "You can." Not because you're so great. But because Christ in you is the greatest.

When the chatterbox says you can't, repeat after Paul: "I can do all things through Him who strengthens me" (Philippians 4:13, NASB).

Opening Question

What are you discouraged about today?

Video Viewing

Watch Video 5, "Discouragement." While watching the video, use the spaces below to record the key points you hear or thoughts you want to remember.

Your Response to the Video

Monologue by the chatterbox

The walls of Jericho falling all at once on the last lap

Abraham in his old age facing the facts without losing faith

If you haven't had a head-on collision with the devil lately, it may be because you're running in the same direction.

Complaining giving a second life to a negative experience

Discouragement as a sign you're advancing in God's plan

Digging down deep, past discouragement

Group Discussion

1. *What challenged you most in Video 5, and why?*

2. This video is the last time we're going to see the chatterbox. He's acting pretty cocky because he thinks he has you discouraged and hopeless.

   What were your thoughts while you listened to the chatterbox deliver his monologue?

3. When we look at what we're facing in life and compare it with what we believe God is calling us to, they don't match up. So discouragement enters our hearts.

   How would you describe the differences between your present reality and your future hopes?

I look at what God has said, and I match it up with what I see. The two don't go together, so discouragement comes in.

4. Read Joshua 6:1–21, the story of an unorthodox siege.

The gates of Jericho were securely barred because of the Israelites. No one went out and no one came in.

Then the LORD said to Joshua, "See, I have delivered Jericho into your hands, along with its king and its fighting men. March around the city once with all the armed men. Do this for six days. Have seven priests carry trumpets of rams' horns in front of the ark. On the seventh day, march around the city seven times, with the priests blowing the trumpets. When you hear them sound a long blast on the trumpets, have the whole army give a loud shout; then the wall of the city will collapse and the army will go up, everyone straight in."

So Joshua son of Nun called the priests and said to them, "Take up the ark of the covenant of the LORD and have seven priests carry trumpets in front of it." And he ordered the army, "Advance! March around the city, with an armed guard going ahead of the ark of the LORD."

When Joshua had spoken to the people, the seven priests carrying the seven trumpets before the LORD went forward, blowing their trumpets, and the ark of the LORD's covenant followed them. The armed guard marched ahead of the priests who blew the trumpets, and the rear guard followed the ark. All this time the trumpets were sounding. But Joshua had commanded the army, "Do not give a war cry, do not raise your voices, do not say a word until the day I tell you to shout. Then shout!" So he had the ark of the LORD carried around the city, circling it once. Then the army returned to camp and spent the night there.

Joshua got up early the next morning and the priests took up the ark of the LORD. The seven priests carrying the seven trumpets went forward, marching before the ark of the LORD and blowing the trumpets. The armed men went ahead of them and the rear guard followed the ark of the LORD, while the trumpets kept sounding. So on the second day they marched around the city once and returned to the camp. They did this for six days.

On the seventh day, they got up at daybreak and marched around the city seven times in the same

When you stop short of complete obedience, when you allow the discouragement to tell you it's not changing, you're relying on your sense rather than activating your spirit.

manner, except that on that day they circled the city seven times. The seventh time around, when the priests sounded the trumpet blast, Joshua commanded the army, "Shout! For the LORD has given you the city! The city and all that is in it are to be devoted to the LORD. Only Rahab the prostitute and all who are with her in her house shall be spared, because she hid the spies we sent. But keep away from the devoted things, so that you will not bring about your own destruction by taking any of them. Otherwise you will make the camp of Israel liable to destruction and bring trouble on it. All the silver and gold and the articles of bronze and iron are sacred to the LORD and must go into his treasury."

When the trumpets sounded, the army shouted, and at the sound of the trumpet, when the men gave a loud shout, the wall collapsed; so everyone charged straight in, and they took the city. They devoted the city to the LORD and destroyed with the sword every living thing in it—men and women, young and old, cattle, sheep and donkeys.

Joshua could easily have become discouraged during those first six days while he and the people were marching around the seemingly impenetrable city of Jericho. But he kept going until the seventh day, and all at once God brought down the walls.

What lap are you on in your battle against a discouraging enemy? Explain.

What might you lose out on if you give up too quickly on God's promises to you?

5. Read Romans 4:18–21, where we learn how Abraham reacted to the seeming contradiction between his own advanced age and God's promise to make him a father.

   Against all hope, Abraham in hope believed and so became the father of many nations, just as it had been said to him, "So shall your offspring be." Without weakening in his faith, he faced the fact that his body was as good as dead—since he was about a hundred years old—and that Sarah's womb was also dead.

Yet he did not waver through unbelief regarding the promise of God, but was strengthened in his faith and gave glory to God, being fully persuaded that God had power to do what he had promised.

"Without weakening in his faith, he faced the fact…" What an example to learn from the father of our faith!

What does it mean for you to face the facts in a current discouraging situation? What does it mean to keep the faith?

6. Complaining kills contentment. On the other hand, gratitude (in addition to giving God honor) serves as a form of self-encouragement.

Don't let what you expected keep you from what God wants you to experience.

What destructive effects of complaining have you seen? Give an example.

How have gratitude and a positive attitude helped you to drown out the voices of discouragement inside your head?

7. God can make a miracle out of any mess. That's why we need to take a second look at our messes. Staying thankful for God's favor, despite our messes, gives us hope while we're waiting for a miracle to come our way.

What are some things you can be grateful to God for today?

8. Many times it's not what happens to us that discourages us; it's our *interpretation* of what happens to us that discourages us. Consider what is most discouraging in your life, then answer…

How does it look to you right now? How might God turn it into something very different in His time?

9. We'd like to think that as we mature in Christ, we should get a free pass from hardship. But, in fact, our battles usually become fiercer.

Would you say that your spiritual life has gotten harder, easier, or stayed the same over time? Explain.

10. Usually our biggest discouragements are not about God's ability to do great things but about our God-given ability to do what He has called us to. That's

why Paul told Timothy to "guard the good deposit" in him (see 2 Timothy 1:6–14). Peter started to doubt his ability to walk on water, and that's when he started to sink (see Matthew 14:25–31).

Do you have doubts about the potential God has put in you? If so, why?

11. When we're discouraged, we shouldn't tap out or try to muscle our way through it in our own strength. Instead, we should dig beneath it, looking for a solid foundation to build our trust on. As Christ's parable of the two builders shows, He and His teachings provide that foundation (see Matthew 7:24–27).

I'm not going to be discouraged about the progress I haven't made, because even my struggle is a sign that I haven't been conquered yet.

What could you do to build your life on Christ more solidly so that you can weather the storms of discouragement?

Closing Prayer

Go around the group and offer encouragement to each other about the troubling situations in your lives. Then pray, turning over your cares to God.

AFTER THE SESSION

Use the following devotional guide and suggested action step to help make the key idea of Session 5 more personal and productive in your life.

My Time with God

Read 2 Corinthians 4, where the apostle Paul shows a resilience in his calling that won't give in to the bad news in his life:

> Since through God's mercy we have this ministry, we do not lose heart. Rather, we have renounced secret and shameful ways; we do not use deception, nor do we distort the word of God. On the contrary, by setting forth the truth plainly we commend ourselves to everyone's conscience in the sight of God. And even if our gospel is veiled, it is veiled to those who are perishing. The god of this age has blinded the minds of unbelievers, so that they cannot see the light of the gospel that displays the glory of Christ, who is the image of God. For what we preach is not ourselves, but Jesus Christ as Lord, and ourselves as your servants for Jesus' sake. For God, who said, "Let light shine out of darkness," made his light shine in our hearts to give us the light of the knowledge of God's glory displayed in the face of Christ.
>
> But we have this treasure in jars of clay to show that this

all-surpassing power is from God and not from us. We are hard pressed on every side, but not crushed; perplexed, but not in despair; persecuted, but not abandoned; struck down, but not destroyed. We always carry around in our body the death of Jesus, so that the life of Jesus may also be revealed in our body. For we who are alive are always being given over to death for Jesus' sake, so that his life may also be revealed in our mortal body. So then, death is at work in us, but life is at work in you.

It is written: "I believed; therefore I have spoken." Since we have that same spirit of faith, we also believe and therefore speak, because we know that the one who raised the Lord Jesus from the dead will also raise us with Jesus and present us with you to himself. All this is for your benefit, so that the grace that is reaching more and more people may cause thanksgiving to overflow to the glory of God.

Therefore we do not lose heart. Though outwardly we are wasting away, yet inwardly we are being renewed day by day. For our light and momentary troubles are achieving for us an eternal glory that far outweighs them all. So we fix our eyes not on what is seen, but on what is unseen, since what is seen is temporary, but what is unseen is eternal.

The gospel is an eternal treasure. Yet we spread this gospel to the world with the help of human bodies, which are as vulnerable as brittle clay jars.

Consider these personal reflection questions:

- *If I were to write my own catalog of weaknesses and obstacles, what would it include?*
- *What was sustaining Paul's hope? What is sustaining mine?*
- *What does this passage teach me about the changes I still need to make in my attitude toward discouraging events in my life?*

Spend time in prayer talking to God about your areas of discouragement and your desire to live out what He has called you to do. Ask Him to give you the same kind of invincible hope that Paul had.

Journal your thoughts here:

My Action Step

Gratitude is a powerful antidote to discouragement. Make a list of your top ten reasons for gratitude to God. If you have trouble coming up with ten good ones, you might ask a good friend or family member to help you. (Sometimes others can see the blessings in our lives better than we can.)

10. _____

9. _____

8. _____

7. _____

6. _____

5. _____

4. _____

3. _____

2. _____

1. _____

Refer to this list whenever discouragement is dragging you down, and use it to inspire prayers of thankfulness to God. It will lift your spirit and give you the determination to go on.

Closing

Crashing the Chatterbox

This session's key idea: Through God's power we can have the ultimate victory in the battle with our thoughts.

####

Chatter fills our minds every day, and it's not going away anytime soon. Yet everything changes when we realize God has given us the ability to choose the dialogue we believe and respond to. And once we learn how, we can switch from lies to truth as deliberately as we can choose the Beatles over Miley Cyrus on satellite radio.

Choosing to believe this, moment by moment, and to act on it is the most important habit we will ever develop. It's the key to pressing ahead and doing God's will even when we are bombarded with thoughts, feelings, and facts about why we can't do it.

I hope by now you are starting to realize that you can access the power of God's promises to constantly crash the system of your broken beliefs. I hope you're learning how to overpower the shouts of the Enemy by tuning in to the whisper of God's truths about your identity in Him and His strength in you.

This war of words will never stop. I know you are tired. I know you have fought many of these battles before and often lost. But now you can decide to never stop crashing the chatterbox.

It will not require your strength or power to win the war, because, thankfully, spiritual warfare isn't hand-to-hand combat. God has given us supernatural weapons that have divine power over the falsehood that sabotages our lives. We crash the chatterbox by launching a counterattack, using the advantage we have as God's children: heaven's perspective.

Opening Question

Where do you stand today as a chatterboxer? Are you feeling weary? defeated? triumphant? Explain.

Video Viewing

Watch Video 6, "Closing." While watching the video, use the spaces below to record the key points you hear or thoughts you want to remember.

Your Response to the Video

The usual defiance

Fighting the chatterbox with the weapons of God's promises

The guarantee of victory

Group Discussion

1. *What challenged you most in Video 6, and why?*

2. Read 1 Samuel 17, the story of God using a teenage boy to bring down a giant who had already paralyzed an army of grown men. Note the *usual* defiance Goliath gave and the *unusual* reaction David had to it.

   Early in the morning David left the flock in the care of a shepherd, loaded up and set out, as Jesse had directed. He reached the camp as the army was going out to its battle positions, shouting the war cry. Israel and the Philistines were drawing up their lines facing each other. David left his things with the keeper of supplies, ran to the battle lines and asked his brothers how they were. As he was talking with them, Goliath, the Philistine champion from Gath, stepped out from his lines and shouted his usual defiance, and David heard it. Whenever the Israelites saw the man, they all fled from him in great fear.

   Now the Israelites had been saying, "Do you see how this man keeps coming out? He comes out to defy

Israel. The king will give great wealth to the man who kills him. He will also give him his daughter in marriage and will exempt his family from taxes in Israel."

David asked the men standing near him, "What will be done for the man who kills this Philistine and removes this disgrace from Israel? Who is this uncircumcised Philistine that he should defy the armies of the living God?"…

What David said was overheard and reported to Saul, and Saul sent for him.

David said to Saul, "Let no one lose heart on account of this Philistine; your servant will go and fight him."

Saul replied, "You are not able to go out against this Philistine and fight him; you are only a young man, and he has been a warrior from his youth."

But David said to Saul, "Your servant has been keeping his father's sheep. When a lion or a bear came

When you've defeated the chatterbox once, you have the capacity to beat it every time. The key is persistence.

*and carried off a sheep from the flock, I went after it,
struck it and rescued the sheep from its mouth. When
it turned on me, I seized it by its hair, struck it and
killed it. Your servant has killed both the lion and the
bear; this uncircumcised Philistine will be like one of
them, because he has defied the armies of the living
God. The LORD who rescued me from the paw of the
lion and the paw of the bear will rescue me from the
hand of this Philistine."*

*Saul said to David, "Go, and the LORD be with
you." (verses 20–26, 31–37)*

Goliath, the giant, shouted ridicule and mockery at the
Israelite forces. It caused most of the men to back down.
It caused David to charge forward.

*After all the discussions we've had, are you feeling
more confident about confronting insecurity, fear,
condemnation, and discouragement in your life? Why
or why not?*

In what areas of your life are you hanging back? In what areas are you rushing into battle?

3. Next, read the section of the story where God, acting through David, silenced Goliath. On one side there was Goliath, the giant, encased in bronze armor and armed with a javelin, a spear, and a shield. And on the other there was David, holding a leather sling and five smooth stones.

   The Philistine, with his shield bearer in front of him, kept coming closer to David. He looked David over and saw that he was little more than a boy, glowing with health and handsome, and he despised him. He said to David, "Am I a dog, that you come at me with sticks?" And the Philistine cursed David by his gods. "Come here," he said, "and I'll give your flesh to the birds and the wild animals!"

   David said to the Philistine, "You come against me with sword and spear and javelin, but I come against you in the name of the LORD Almighty, the God of the armies of Israel, whom you have defied.

This day the LORD will deliver you into my hands,
and I'll strike you down and cut off your head. This
very day I will give the carcasses of the Philistine army
to the birds and the wild animals, and the whole
world will know that there is a God in Israel. All those
gathered here will know that it is not by sword or spear
that the LORD saves; for the battle is the LORD's, and
he will give all of you into our hands."

As the Philistine moved closer to attack him,
David ran quickly toward the battle line to meet him.
Reaching into his bag and taking out a stone, he slung
it and struck the Philistine on the forehead. The stone
sank into his forehead, and he fell facedown on the
ground.

So David triumphed over the Philistine with
a sling and a stone; without a sword in his hand he
struck down the Philistine and killed him. (verses
41–50)

David didn't go near Goliath. The giant's advantage in
hand-to-hand combat would have overwhelmed him.
Instead, David used his skill as a projectile warrior to
launch a rock from a distance. In the same way, we
have to use unconventional weaponry in our war to
quiet the chatter. Reread 2 Corinthians 10:3–5, a
passage we looked at back in Session 1:

Though we live in the world, we do not wage war as the world does. The weapons we fight with are not the weapons of the world. On the contrary, they have divine power to demolish strongholds. We demolish arguments and every pretension that sets itself up against the knowledge of God, and we take captive every thought to make it obedient to Christ.

"Take captive every thought"—that's chatterbox-crashing language. And note that it requires supernatural weaponry.

How have you seen that your own strength, determination, or willpower is inadequate to defeat the chatterbox?

Every victory you win means another battle you will have to fight.

*How have you seen the power of God in you defeat
the lies?*

*What are the supernatural weapons that can aid you
in your battle to get control over the chatterbox?*

4. God's promises in Scripture assure us that He is on our
   side. Consider these promises to be the rocks for your
   sling against the giant you face: the chatterbox.

   *What promises of God are most meaningful to you in
   your battles with the chatterbox?*

5. Your mind will always be a factory for chatter. But now you know how to manage the output.

What are the most important lessons you have learned about crashing the chatterbox? Describe the progress you have already made in the following areas:

Insecurity

Fear

What sets us apart now is that, instead of backing down when we hear the voice of the chatterbox, we charge forward in God's strength.

Condemnation

Discouragement

What chatterbox-crashing lessons do you still need to apply in your life?

What questions or concerns do you still have about crashing the chatterbox?

6. Jesus said, "In this world you will have trouble. But take heart! I have overcome the world" (John 16:33). We need to fight from this perspective, relying on Christ. If we do, victory is guaranteed.

What might victory look like for you?

Closing Prayer

At the end of Video 6, Pastor Furtick prays,

> God, would You bless the men and women and the boys and girls who have participated in this experience to know that Your promises and Your Word and the thoughts that You think toward us are more powerful than anything that the Enemy will bring against us. We thank You that Your word is the last word, the first word, and the sustaining word in every season of our lives. In every insecurity, every fear, through all of our shame and discouragement, You are faithful, and we will win this war as we stand on Your promises. In Jesus's name, amen.

In the same spirit, add your own prayers of thankfulness, praise, or request.

Use the following devotional guide and suggested action step to help make the key idea of Session 6 more personal and productive in your life.

My Time with God

When David brought down Goliath with a stone to the giant's forehead, it was just the first of many fights for David. Late in his life he wrote a song of praise "when the LORD delivered him from the hand of all his enemies" (2 Samuel 22:1). Read the following portion of this song (which also appears in the Bible as Psalm 18:30–42):

> *As for God, his way is perfect:*
> *The LORD's word is flawless;*
> *he shields all who take refuge in him.*
> *For who is God besides the LORD?*
> *And who is the Rock except our God?*
> *It is God who arms me with strength*
> *and keeps my way secure.*
> *He makes my feet like the feet of a deer;*
> *he causes me to stand on the heights.*
> *He trains my hands for battle;*
> *my arms can bend a bow of bronze.*
> *You make your saving help my shield;*
> *your help has made me great.*

You provide a broad path for my feet,
  so that my ankles do not give way.

I pursued my enemies and crushed them;
  I did not turn back till they were destroyed.
I crushed them completely, and they could not rise;
  they fell beneath my feet.
You armed me with strength for battle;
  you humbled my adversaries before me.
You made my enemies turn their backs in flight,
  and I destroyed my foes.
They cried for help, but there was no one to save
        them—
  to the LORD, but he did not answer.
I beat them as fine as the dust of the earth;
  I pounded and trampled them like mud in the streets.
        (2 Samuel 22:31–43)

David's enemies went down in defeat before him. And in the same way, our enemy the chatterbox is ultimately destined to lose. God gives the victory.

Consider these personal reflection questions:
- *How has the Lord been training me for the battle against lies?*
- *If I were to compose a song of praise to God about my victories, what would it refer to?*

- *How is my enthusiasm for fighting the chatterbox holding up?*

Ask the Lord to strengthen you to fight the good fight against the chatter for the rest of your life. Pray for Him to deliver you in the end from all the lies that threaten you.

Journal your thoughts here:

My Action Step

One of the most important things to have in the war of words with the chatterbox is an ally, someone who will help you fight and who will also ask for your support when he or she needs it. God can often strengthen and encourage you through others. So ask yourself, *Whom can I help crash the chatterbox in their lives? Who can help me?*

If you have felt particularly drawn to another member of the discussion group, contact him or her and talk about keeping in touch to encourage each other in your efforts to follow Christ faithfully. Or perhaps there is someone else in your life who could fulfill that role.

My desired chatterboxing partner: _____

Work together and see what the Lord will do for you both. This is how it goes:

    God says I am. *CRASH!*
    God says He will. *CRASH! CRASH!*
    God says He has. *CRASH! CRASH! CRASH!*
    God says I can. *CRASH! CRASH! CRASH! CRASH!*

Leader's Helps

Being the leader of a group using the *Crash the Chatterbox Participant's Guide* isn't hard work. It's mainly a process of facilitating the discussion. Yet if you're willing to take on that leadership role, it will give you a chance to help the group members experience the victory in their thought lives that God wants them to have. So make the most of it.

Tips for the Group Leader

- Think about how you might want to promote your *Crash the Chatterbox* discussion group. For example, do you want to schedule a presentation at your church? Make sure that everyone who chooses to take part in the group has a copy of *Crash the Chatterbox* as well as a copy of this participant's guide. Encourage them to read the introduction and the first chapter of *Crash the Chatterbox* before coming to the first session. Gather phone numbers or e-mail addresses so you can communicate with the participants. Send them a reminder of when and where the first session will be held.

- Watch the video and work through the participant's guide session on your own each week before your group gets together. Think through the key points—what they mean to you and what they might mean to your group members. Pray for God to work in you and in your group.

- Decide if you're going to have refreshments, and if so, arrange for someone to provide them, or provide them yourself.

- Arrive at the meeting location ahead of time to ensure you have everything you need. Test the video equipment with the DVD. Have some Bibles, pens, and notepaper on hand. You may also need a white board. Check to see that the seating, lighting, room temperature, and so on are suitable for a comfortable conversation.

- Welcome everyone who shows up. Introduce participants to each other if they're not already acquainted. Prepare an icebreaker for the beginning of at least the first session to help people feel more comfortable with one another.

- Take personal prayer requests, either at the beginning or end of each session, and lead the group in prayer.

- During the group discussion time, ask the questions aloud. If some participants seem as though they would like to say more but are hesitant, try to gently draw them out. If others are monopolizing the group's time, politely interrupt them and redirect the conversation. Feel free to add to or adapt the questions in the participant's guide to personalize the discussion for your group. Monitor the progress of the conversation to make sure you can cover all the important points in the time available. Yet if it seems that God is doing something special in the group, just go with it, even if it means deviating from your original plan.

- Encourage group members to use the After the Session sections on their own at home. You may wish to check in with them via text or e-mail during the week.

- At your final session, invite your group to go to crashthechatterbox.com to discover additional resources related to overcoming the chatterbox.

ABOUT THE AUTHOR

Steven Furtick is a *New York Times* best-selling author and the founder and lead pastor of Elevation Church, a multisite church based in Charlotte, North Carolina. He has been privileged to minister to a global audience, speaking at conferences and churches around the world. He holds a master of divinity degree from Southern Baptist Theological Seminary. He and his wife, Holly, live in the Charlotte area with their three children: Elijah, Graham, and Abbey.

The Voice You Listen to Will Determine the Future You Experience

Discover the core book behind the study. Learn how to live out God's truth no matter what is going on in your life or thoughts. Learn how to crash the chatterbox…and hear God's voice above all others.

Also from Steven Furtick!

In *Greater*, Pastor Steven Furtick draws on the biblical story of Elisha to give you the confidence to know that nothing is impossible with God, the clarity to see the next step He's calling you to take, and the courage to do anything He tells you to do.

> **DVD and participant's guide for individual or small group use also available.**

Read an excerpt from this book and more at
www.WaterBrookMultnomah.com!